Dear Sheri and
Joe,
When I saw this book, I just
couldn't resist it. It teaches
profound truths through
little people —
But that's
what children
do best,
isn't it?

They
really
in
so many
ways,
teach us.

Enjoy your
new miracle!
With love,
Jim and
Barb
Miller

BEHOLD YOUR LITTLE ONES

Toni Sorenson Brown

FOR ALL CHILDREN

*Special thanks to the children who participated
and to the parents who love them.*

*And much gratitude to
"The Committee."*

Published by Covenant Communications, Inc. American Fork, Utah

Cover design © 2005 by Covenant Communications, Inc.
Copyright © 2005 Toni Sorenson Brown

Printed in China
First Printing: August 2005

12 11 10 09 08 07 06 05   10 9 8 7 6 5 4 3 2 1

ISBN 1-59156-567-7

. . . he took their little children,
one by one, and blessed them,
and prayed unto the Father for them....
And he spake unto the multitude,
and said unto them:
Behold your little ones.

3 NE. 17:21, 23

We lived in the presence of God in the spirit
before we came here.
We desired to be like him,
we saw him, we were in his presence.

JOSEPH FIELDING SMITH, *Doctrines of Salvation,* ED. BRUCE R. MCCONKIE (SALT LAKE CITY:BOOKCRAFT, 1954–1956), 1:56

As man is, God once was;
and as God is, man may become.

LORENZO SNOW (SPENCER W. KIMBALL, "OUR GREAT POTENTIAL," *Ensign,* MAY 1977, 49)

belly I knew thee.

JER 1:5

How WONDERFUL a thing
is a child. How beautiful is
a NEWBORN BABE. There is
NO GREATER MIRACLE
than the CREATION of human life.

GORDON B. HINCKLEY
"WHAT ARE PEOPLE ASKING ABOUT US?" Ensign, NOV. 1998, 70

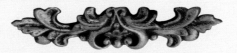

He WINKETH with his eyes,

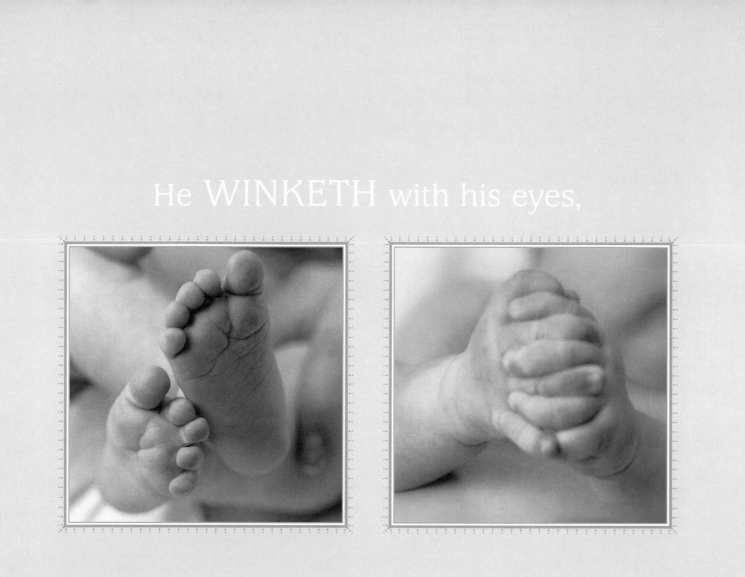

he SPEAKETH with his feet,

he TEACHETH with his fingers.

Every spirit of man was innocent in the beginning .

D&C 93:38

I wonder sometimes

as I travel throughout the country and see the

hundreds of thousands of people

scattered everywhere, how many of them there are

that realize that they are the children of the Lord.

He is the Father of our spirits.

GEORGE ALBERT SMITH, *Teachings of the Presidents of the Church*

I THOUGHT OF
THE **MIRACLE** OF
CHILDREN
WHO BECOME THE
WORLD'S CONSTANT
RENEWAL
OF **LIFE** AND
PURPOSE.

GORDON B. HINCKLEY,
"BEHOLD YOUR LITTLE ONES,"
Ensign, NOV. 1978, 18

You are to be

the ROYAL ARMY of the Lord

in the last days.

You are

"YOUTH OF THE

NOBLE BIRTHRIGHT."

EZRA TAFT BENSON, "TO THE 'YOUTH OF THE NOBLE BIRTHRIGHT,'" *Ensign*, MAY 1986

These I will

make my rulers

ABR. 3:23

THE SECRET OF A HAPPY MARRIAGE IS TO SERVE GOD AND EACH OTHER.

EZRA TAFT BENSON, "FUNDAMENTALS OF ENDURING FAMILY RELATIONSHIPS," Ensign, NOV. 1982, 60

*M*arriage is perhaps the most vital of all the decisions and has the most far-reaching effects, for it has to do not only with immediate happiness, but also with eternal joys. It affects not only the two people involved, but also their families and particularly their children and their children's children down through the many generations.

SPENCER W. KIMBALL, "ONENESS IN MARRIAGE," Ensign, MAR. 1977, 3

...ye have received the

SPIRIT OF ADOPTION,

whereby we cry, Abba, Father.

ROM. 8:15

Adoption is an
UNSELFISH, LOVING DECISION
that blesses both
the birth parents and
the children in this life
and in eternity.

GORDON B. HINCKLEY, *letter from First Presidency,* JUNE 26, 2002

Behold, I send an *Angel* before thee, to keep thee in *the way* and to bring thee into the place which *I* have prepared.

EX. 23:20

Heaven was in our home.

SPENCER W. KIMBALL, "THEREFORE I WAS TAUGHT," *Ensign*, JAN. 1982, 3

CHILDREN
SEALED TO PARENTS
HAVE CLAIM UPON THE
BLESSINGS OF THE GOSPEL
BEYOND WHAT
OTHERS ARE ENTITLED
TO RECEIVE.

GORDON B. HINCKLEY,
letter from First Presidency, JUNE 26, 2002

WE HAVE COMMITTED TO OUR CARE

pearls of great price.

WE HAVE BECOME THE *fathers and mothers of lives,*

AND THE GODS OF THE HOLY PRIESTHOOD IN *the eternal worlds* HAVE BEEN WATCHING US . . .

JOHN TAYLOR, *Journal of Discourses,* 20:60–61

WITH THE ARRIVAL OF THE FIRST CHILD
THE PARENTS MUST MAKE DECISIONS ABOUT
HOW TO TEACH AND TRAIN,
HOW TO CORRECT AND DISCIPLINE.

HOWARD W. HUNTER, "PARENTS' CONCERN FOR CHILDREN," *Ensign*, NOV. 1983, 63

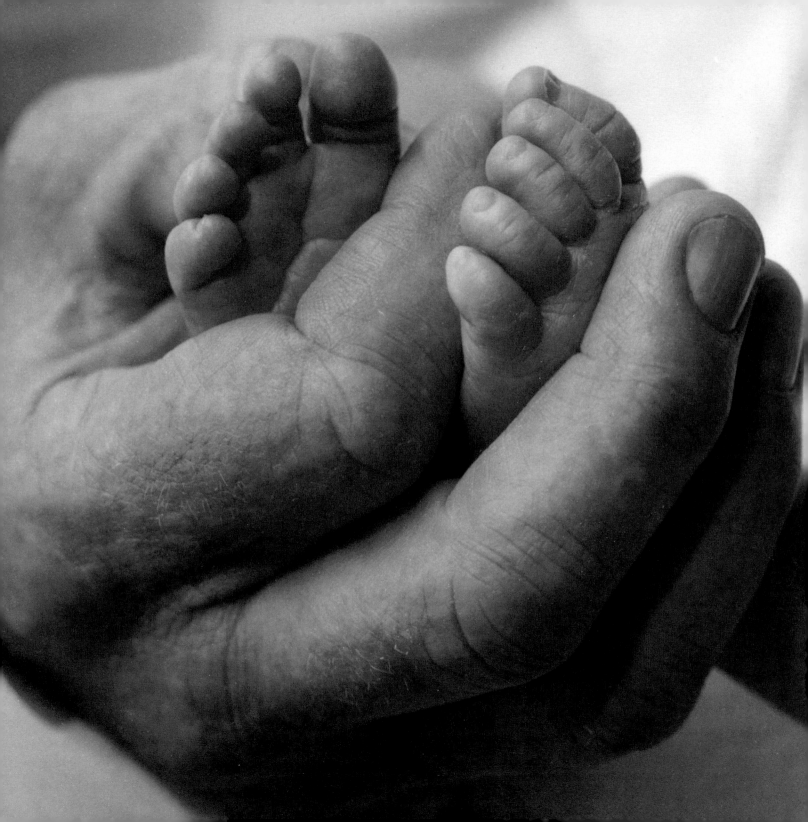

THE RESPONSIBILITIES OF
PARENTHOOD ARE OF THE
GREATEST IMPORTANCE. THE RESULTS OF
OUR EFFORTS WILL HAVE ETERNAL
CONSEQUENCES FOR US
AND THE BOYS AND GIRLS WE RAISE.

HOWARD W. HUNTER, "PARENTS' CONCERN FOR CHILDREN," *Ensign*, NOV. 1983, 63

How wonderful it is to know that he is not far from us, that he is all-powerful,
and has promised us that if trouble comes, if necessary, he will come down in heaven,
not *from* heaven, he will bring heaven with him upon this earth and fight our battles
and preserve us, and we will go on living throughout the ages of eternity.
That is the promise of our Heavenly Father.

GEORGE ALBERT SMITH

AND WE TALK OF *Christ* ...

THAT OUR CHILDREN MAY KNOW

to what source they may look

FOR A REMISSION OF THEIR SINS.

2 NE. 25:26

ANYONE WHO *becomes a parent*

IS UNDER STRICT OBLIGATION TO

protect and love HIS CHILDREN

AND ASSIST THEM TO

return to their Heavenly Father.

HOWARD W. HUNTER,
"PARENTS' CONCERN FOR CHILDREN," *Ensign*, NOV. 1983, 63

If you are ever called upon to chasten a person,

never chasten beyond the balm

you have within you to bind up.

BRIGHAM YOUNG, Journal of Discourses, 9:125

BRING UP YOUR CHILDREN IN
THE LOVE AND FEAR OF THE LORD;
STUDY THEIR DISPOSITIONS AND THEIR
TEMPERAMENTS, AND DEAL WITH THEM ACCORDINGLY,
NEVER ALLOWING YOURSELF TO CORRECT THEM
IN THE HEAT OF PASSION; TEACH THEM TO
LOVE YOU RATHER THAN TO FEAR YOU.

BRIGHAM YOUNG, Journal of Discourses, 19:222

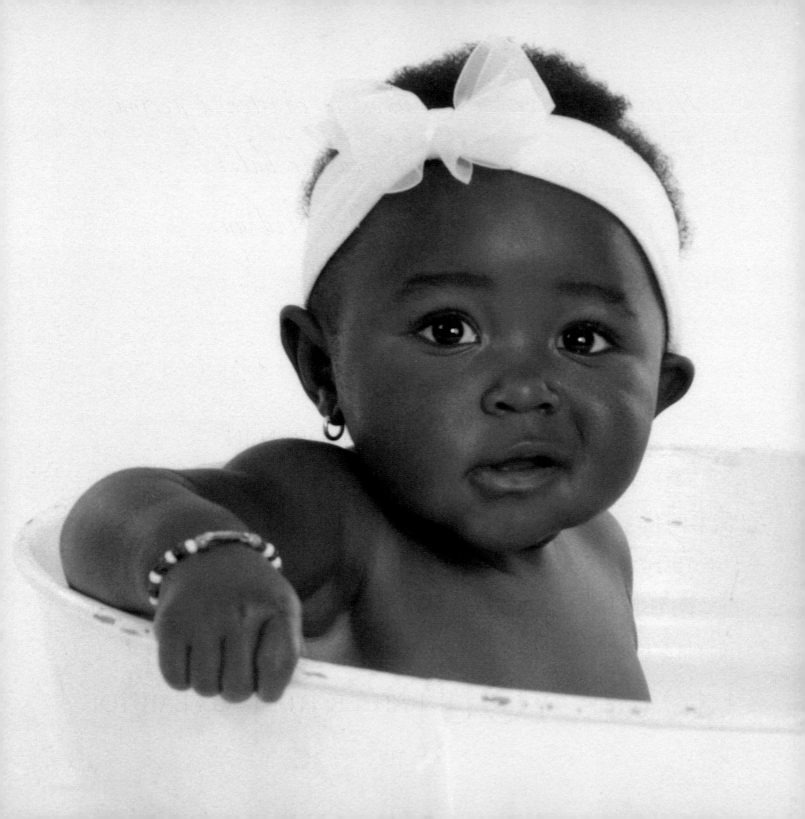

YOU PARENTS,
LOVE YOUR CHILDREN...
YOU NEED MORE THAN YOUR
OWN WISDOM IN REARING THEM.
YOU NEED THE HELP OF THE LORD.
PRAY FOR THAT HELP AND
FOLLOW THE INSPIRATION
WHICH YOU RECEIVE.

GORDON B. HINCKLEY, "THE FABRIC OF FAITH AND TESTIMONY," *Ensign*, NOV. 1995, 89

COUNSEL WITH THE LORD IN ALL THY DOINGS,
AND HE WILL DIRECT THEE FOR GOOD

ALMA 37:37

INASMUCH AS YE

HAVE DONE IT

UNTO ONE OF THE

LEAST OF THESE . . .

YE HAVE DONE IT

UNTO ME.

MATT. 25:40

BECAUSE PARENTS HAVE DEPARTED FROM THE PRINCIPLES THE LORD GAVE FOR HAPPINESS AND SUCCESS, FAMILIES THROUGH-OUT THE WORLD ARE UNDERGOING GREAT STRESS AND TRAUMA.

EZRA TAFT BENSON, *Love* (SALT LAKE CITY: DESERET BOOK CO., 1986), 1

Lo, children are an heritage of the Lord.

PS. 127:3

A successful parent is
one who has loved,
one who has sacrificed, and
one who has cared for,
taught, and ministered to
the needs of a child.
If you have done all of these
and your child is still
wayward or troublesome or
worldly, it could well be
that you are, nevertheless,
a successful parent.

HOWARD W. HUNTER, "PARENTS' CONCERN FOR CHILDREN,"
Ensign, NOV. 1983, 63

YOU SHOULD NEVER SAY A
WORD OR DO AN ACT WHICH
YOU WOULD NOT WANT YOUR
CHILDREN TO COPY AFTER.

JOHN TAYLOR, *Journal of Discourses,* 26:113

ONE OF THE GREAT TEACHINGS OF

the Man of Galilee, THE LORD JESUS CHRIST,

WAS THAT YOU AND I CARRY WITHIN US

immense possibilities. IN URGING US TO BE PERFECT

AS OUR FATHER IN HEAVEN IS *perfect,* JESUS WAS NOT

TAUNTING US OR TEASING US. HE WAS TELLING US

a powerful truth ABOUT OUR POSSIBILITIES AND

ABOUT OUR POTENTIAL. IT IS A TRUTH ALMOST

too stunning to contemplate.

SPENCER W. KIMBALL, "JESUS: THE PERFECT LEADER," Ensign, AUG. 1979, 5

NEVER FORGET THAT

THESE LITTLE ONES ARE THE

SONS AND DAUGHTERS OF GOD

AND THAT YOURS IS A CUSTODIAL

RELATIONSHIP TO THEM, THAT HE WAS A

PARENT BEFORE YOU WERE PARENTS AND THAT

HE HAS NOT RELINQUISHED HIS PARENTAL

RIGHTS OR INTEREST IN THESE LITTLE ONES.

GORDON B. HINCKLEY, SALT LAKE UNIVERSITY THIRD STAKE CONFERENCE,
3 NOV. 1996 (IN Church News, 1 MAR, 1997, 2)

Feed my

And he gathereth his
children from the four
quarters of the earth;
. . . he shall feed his
sheep, and in him they
shall find pasture.

1 NE. 22: 25

lambs

EACH OF US IS AN INDIVIDUAL.
EACH OF US IS DIFFERENT.
THERE MUST BE RESPECT FOR
THOSE DIFFERENCES. . .

GORDON B. HINCKLEY, *Teachings of Gordon B. Hinckley* (SALT LAKE CITY: DESERET BOOK CO.), 1997, 661

. . .HE DENIETH NONE THAT
COME UNTO HIM, BLACK AND WHITE,
BOND AND FREE, MALE AND FEMALE . . .
ALL ARE ALIKE UNTO GOD.

2 NE. 26:33

And they shall also teach
their children to pray,
and to walk uprightly
before the Lord.

D&C 68:28

Teach them how to approach God,
that they may call upon him
and he will hear them. . .

JOHN TAYLOR, Journal of Discourses, 20:60–61

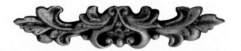

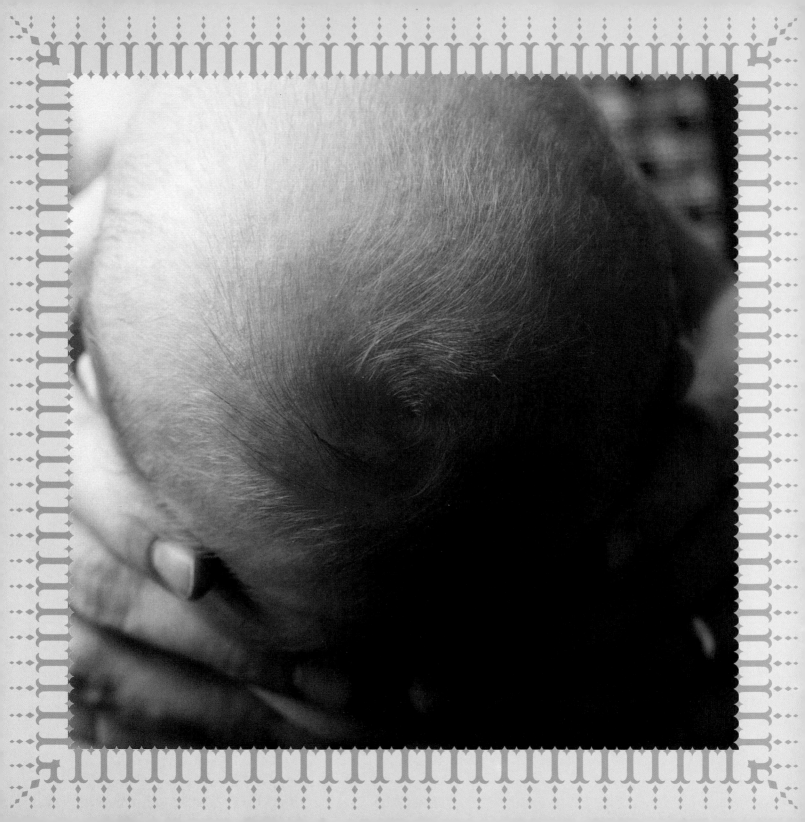

A Father's Blessing

FATHERS, IF YOU WISH YOUR CHILDREN TO BE TAUGHT IN THE PRINCIPLES OF
THE GOSPEL, IF YOU WISH THEM TO LOVE THE TRUTH AND UNDERSTAND IT,
IF YOU WISH THEM TO BE OBEDIENT TO AND UNITED WITH YOU, LOVE THEM!
. . . HOWEVER WAYWARD THEY MIGHT BE . . . WHEN YOU SPEAK OR TALK TO
THEM, DO IT NOT IN ANGER, DO IT NOT HARSHLY, IN A CONDEMNING SPIRIT.
SPEAK TO THEM KINDLY . . . YOU CANNOT DO IT BY DRIVING."

JOSEPH F. SMITH, *Gospel Doctrine: Selections from the Sermons and Writings of Joseph F. Smith.*
COMP. JOHN A. WIDTSOE (SALT LAKE CITY: DESERET BOOK CO., 1939), 316

Choose you this day
whom ye will serve . . .
but as for me
and my house,
we will serve
the Lord.

JOSH. 24:15

YOU NEED NEVER FEEL INFERIOR. YOU NEED NEVER FEEL THAT YOU WERE BORN WITHOUT TALENTS OR WITHOUT OPPORTUNITIES TO GIVE THEM EXPRESSION. CULTIVATE WHATEVER TALENTS YOU HAVE, AND THEY WILL GROW AND REFINE AND BECOME AN EXPRESSION OF YOUR TRUE SELF APPRECIATED BY OTHERS.

GORDON B. HINCKLEY, "THE LIGHT WITHIN YOU," *Ensign*, MAY 1995, 99

. . . LOVE ONE ANOTHER

AS I HAVE LOVED YOU.

JOHN 15:12

The Lord has given [the priesthood] to men who are considered worthy to receive it, regardless of station in life, the color of their skin, or the nation in which they live. It is the power and the authority to govern in the affairs of the kingdom of God.

GORDON B. HINCKLEY, "CORNERSTONE OF OUR FAITH," *Ensign*, NOV. 1984, 5

IF WE TRULY HONOR OUR PARENTS, WE WILL SEEK TO EMULATE THEIR BEST CHARACTERISTICS AND TO FULFILL THEIR HIGHEST ASPIRATIONS FOR US.

SPENCER W. KIMBALL, "HONORING PARENTS AND BEING HONORABLE PARENTS," *Ensign,* JULY 1986, 57

TRAIN UP
A CHILD
IN THE
WAY HE
SHOULD GO;
AND WHEN
HE IS OLD,
HE WILL
NOT DEPART
FROM IT.

PROV. 22:6

. . . . they had been

IN MY OBSERVATION, I HAVE FOUND THAT

MANY MEN WHO HAVE BEEN

SUCCESSFUL IN THE

BATTLE OF LIFE

ARE INDEBTED PRINCIPALLY TO

THE EXAMPLE, THE ENERGY, AND THE

UNTIRING LABORS OF

FAITHFUL MOTHERS.

HEBER J. GRANT

taught by their mothers . . . .

ALMA 56:47

TAKE TIME TO **TRULY LOVE**
YOUR CHILDREN. A MOTHER'S
UNQUALIFIED LOVE APPROACHES
CHRISTLIKE LOVE.

THOMAS S. MONSON, "MEMORIES OF YESTERDAY, COUNSEL FOR TODAY," *Ensign,* MAY 1992, 4

LET EVERY MOTHER
REALIZE THAT SHE HAS
NO GREATER BLESSING
THAN THE CHILDREN WHICH HAVE COME
TO HER AS A GIFT FROM THE ALMIGHTY;
THAT SHE HAS
NO GREATER MISSION
THAN TO REAR THEM IN LIGHT AND TRUTH,
IN UNDERSTANDING AND LOVE . . .

GORDON B. HINCKLEY, "BRING UP A CHILD IN THE WAY HE SHOULD GO," *Ensign,* NOV. 1998, 97

I say to you mothers, if you ever have sons and daughters who amount to what they should in the world, it will be in no small degree due to the fact that your children have a mother who spends many nights on her knees in prayer, praying God that her son, her daughter, will not fail.

HAROLD B. LEE, *The Teachings of Harold B. Lee*, ED. CLYDE J. WILLIAMS (SALT LAKE CITY: BOOKCRAFT, 1996), 286

This ability and willingness to
properly rear children,
the gift to love, and eagerness,
yes, longing to express it
in soul development, make
motherhood the noblest office or
calling in the world . . . She who
can paint a masterpiece or write
a book that will influence
millions deserves the admiration
and the plaudits of mankind; but
she who rears successfully a
family of healthy, beautiful sons
and daughters, whose influence
will be felt through generations
to come, whose immortal souls
will exert an influence through-
out the ages long after paintings
shall have faded, and books and
statues shall have decayed or
shall have been destroyed,
deserves the highest honor that
man can give, and the choicest
blessing of God. In her high duty
and service to humanity,
endowing with immortality
eternal spirits, she is co-partner
with the Creator Himself.

DAVID O. MCKAY, *Gospel Ideals: Selections from the
Discourses of David O. McKay* (SALT LAKE CITY:
IMPROVEMENT ERA, 1953), 453–54

Lengthen Your Stride

SPENCER W. KIMBALL, *The Teachings of Spencer W. Kimball*, ED. EDWARD L. KIMBALL (SALT LAKE CITY: BOOKCRAFT, 1982), 564

My
Brother's
Keeper

A competent mother in every home is the greatest need in the world today.

DAVID O. MCKAY, *Relief Society Magazine*, JAN. 1936, 4. QUOTED IN *LDS Women's Treasury: Insights and Inspiration for Today's Woman* (SALT LAKE CITY: DESERET BOOK CO., 1997), 444

. . . be strong in the Lord, and in the power of his might. Put on the

WHOLE ARMOUR OF GOD,

that ye may be able to stand against the wiles of the devil.

EPH. 6:10–11

Perhaps there are children who have come into the world that would CHALLENGE any set of parents under any set of circumstances.

Likewise, perhaps there are others who would bless the lives of, and BE A JOY to, almost any father or mother.

HOWARD W. HUNTER, "PARENTS' CONCERN FOR CHILDREN," *Ensign,* NOV. 1983, 63

LET THERE BE MUSIC IN THE HOME.

GORDON B. HINCKLEY, *Be Thou an Example* (SALT LAKE CITY: DESERET BOOK CO., 1981)

Praise the Lord with singing, with music, and with dancing.

D&C 136:28

For my soul delighteth in the song of the heart; yea, the song of the righteous is a prayer unto me . . .

D&C 25:12

Teach the Children

Within the revealed gospel of Jesus Christ,
and from the teachings of our Church leaders,
may be found the answers to every
question and the solution of
every problem essential to
the social, temporal, and
spiritual welfare of human
beings who are all the children
of God, our Eternal Father.

HAROLD B. LEE

Ever Learning

. . . see that your young and fruitful minds are fed and stored with good principles. You want to learn that which is true—when you learn anything about God, Jesus Christ, the angels, the Holy Ghost, the gospel, the way to be saved, your duty to your parents, brethren, sisters or to any of your fellow men, or any history, art or science, I say when you learn those things, you want to learn that which is true, so that when you get those things riveted in your mind and planted in your heart, and you trust to it in future life and lean upon it for support, that it may not fail you like a broken reed.

WILFORD WOODRUFF, The Discourses of Wilford Woodruff, ED. G. HOMER DURHAM (SALT LAKE CITY: BOOKCRAFT, 1969), 266

THE GREATEST TRUST
THAT CAN COME TO A
MAN AND WOMAN IS
THE PLACING IN THEIR
KEEPING THE LIFE OF A
LITTLE CHILD.

DAVID O. MCKAY, *Conference Report,* APRIL 1955,
MORNING SESSION, 25–26

The serpent beguiled me, and I did eat.

GEN. 3:13

REARING HAPPY, PEACEFUL CHILDREN
IS NO EASY CHALLENGE IN TODAY'S WORLD,
BUT IT CAN BE DONE,
AND IT IS BEING DONE.

EZRA TAFT BENSON, "SALVATION—A FAMILY AFFAIR," Ensign, JULY 1992, 2

PARENTS, BE TRUTHFUL; LET OUR CHILDREN HAVE
CONFIDENCE IN YOUR WORD, SO THAT IF FATHER OR
MOTHER SAYS ANYTHING, THEY MIGHT SAY, "IF FATHER
OR MOTHER SAYS SUCH AND SUCH A THING, I KNOW IT
IS RIGHT, BECAUSE FATHER OR MOTHER SAID IT, AND
THEY NEVER PREVARICATE OR TELL A FALSEHOOD."
THAT IS THE KIND OF FEELING WE WANT TO CULTIVATE
AMONG OURSELVES AND WITH OUR FAMILIES.

JOHN TAYLOR, Journal of Discourses, 22:317

But in our family circles,

OUR **CHILDREN** WILL LEARN
HOW TO TALK TO THEIR
HEAVENLY FATHER
BY LISTENING TO THEIR PARENTS.

They will soon see how heartfelt and honest our prayers are.

If our prayers are hurried, even tending to be thoughtless ritual, they

will see this also. Better that we do in our families and in private

as Mormon pleaded, "Wherefore, my beloved brethren, pray

unto the Father with all the energy of heart."

(Moroni 7:48)

SPENCER W. KIMBALL, "PRAY ALWAYS," *Ensign*, OCT. 1981, 3

Service

WHEN YE ARE IN THE SERVICE OF YOUR FELLOW BEINGS
YE ARE ONLY IN THE SERVICE OF YOUR GOD.

MOSIAH 2:17

IT IS NOT WHAT WE RECEIVE

THAT ENRICHES OUR LIVES,

IT IS WHAT WE GIVE.

GEORGE ALBERT SMITH, *Conference Report*, APRIL 1935, AFTERNOON MEETING, 46

ABOVE ALL ELSE, CHILDREN NEED TO
KNOW AND FEEL THEY ARE
LOVED, WANTED, AND APPRECIATED.
THEY NEED TO BE
ASSURED OF THAT OFTEN.

EZRA TAFT BENSON, "FUNDAMENTALS OF ENDURING FAMILY RELATIONSHIPS," Ensign, NOV. 1982, 59

CHILDREN TODAY NEED TO BE TAUGHT AS JESUS
TAUGHT—WITH LOVE, UNDERSTANDING, COMPASSION,
AND PATIENCE. NO EFFORT IS TOO GREAT; NO LABOR
MORE WORTHWHILE.

SPENCER W. KIMBALL, "TRAIN UP A CHILD," Ensign, APR. 1978, 2

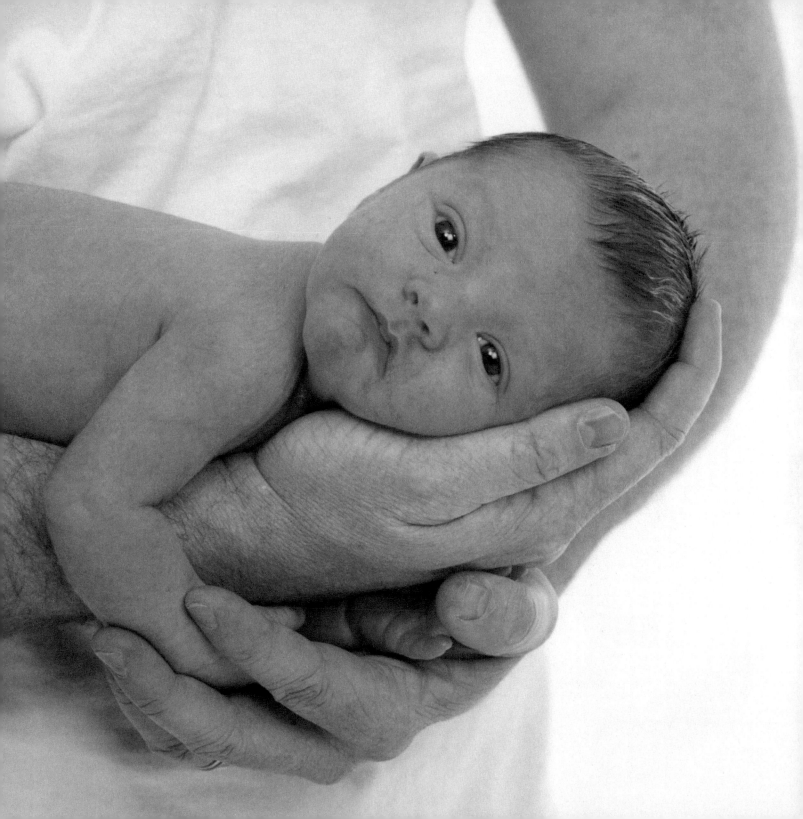

Thy word is a lamp unto my feet,
and a light unto my path.

PS. 119:105

Teach your sons and daughters to do their best and not be satisfied with something mediocre.

GEORGE ALBERT SMITH

I promise you that if you will keep your

JOURNALS AND RECORDS,

they will indeed be a source of

GREAT INSPIRATION

to your families,

to your children,

your grandchildren,

and others, on through

the generations.

SPENCER W. KIMBALL, "PRESIDENT KIMBALL SPEAKS OUT ON PERSONAL JOURNALS," *Ensign.* DEC. 1980, 60

One of the most serious human defects in all ages is procrastination.

SPENCER W. KIMBALL, *The Teachings of Spencer W. Kimball*, ED. EDWARD L. KIMBALL
(SALT LAKE CITY: BOOKCRAFT, 1982), 48

Let us teach our children while they are yet young of the great opportunity and responsibility of paying tithing. If we do so, there will be another generation, and yet another, who will walk in the ways of the Lord and merit His promised blessings.

GORDON B. HINCKLEY, "LOOK TO THE FUTURE," Ensign, NOV. 1997, 67

Search . . .

Ponder . . .

and Pray.

For my soul delighteth in
the scriptures, and my
heart pondereth them,
and writeth them for the
learning and the profit of
my children.

2 NE. 4:15

Read to your children.

Read the story of the Son of God.

Read to them from the New Testament.

Read to them from the Book of Mormon.

It will take time, and you are very busy,

but it will prove to be a great blessing in your lives

as well as their lives.

And there will grow in their hearts

a great love for the Savior of the world,

the only perfect man who walked the earth.

He will become to them a very real living being,

and His great atoning sacrifice as they grow

to manhood and womanhood,

will take on a new and more

glorious meaning in their lives.

GORDON B. HINCKLEY, (QUOTED IN Church News, 6 DEC. 1997, 2)

God has saved for
THE FINAL INNING
some of His stronger and
most valiant children,
who will help bear off
the kingdom triumphantly.

EZRA TAFT BENSON, "NEWS OF THE CHURCH,"
Ensign, APRIL 1987, 73

Hold to
the Rod

A child who sees his father active in the Church, serving God through service to his fellowman, will likely act in the same spirit when he or she grows up. A child who sees his mother assisting those in distress, succoring the poor, and going to the rescue of those in trouble will likely exemplify that same spirit as he or she grows in years.

GORDON B. HINCKLEY, "THE ENVIRONMENT OF OUR HOMES," *Ensign,* JUNE 1985, 3

God is good. He is eager to forgive. He wants us to perfect ourselves and maintain control of ourselves. He does not want Satan and others to control our lives. We must learn that keeping our Heavenly Father's commandments represents the *only* path to total control of ourselves, the only way to find joy, truth, and fulfillment in this life and in eternity.

SPENCER W. KIMBALL, "THE GOSPEL OF REPENTANCE," *Ensign*, OCT. 1982, 2

Blessed are the

peacemakers: for they

shall be called the

children of God.

MATT. 5:9

Little children do have

words given unto

them many

times, which

confound the

wise and the

learned.

ALMA 32:23

. . . we will build up and establish Zion, and roll forth that kingdom which God has designed shall rule and reign over the nations of the earth. We want to PREPARE them for these things; and to STUDY from the best books as well as by FAITH, and become acquainted with the LAWS of nations, and of kingdoms and governments, and with everything calculated to exalt, ennoble, and DIGNIFY THE HUMAN FAMILY.

JOHN TAYLOR, *Journal of Discourses,* 26 VOLS. (LONDON: LATTER-DAY SAINTS' BOOK DEPOT, 1854–1886), 20: 60–61

. . . none shall be
found blameless before
God, except it be little
children . . .

MOSIAH 3:21

Man shall not live
by bread alone,
but by every word
that prodeedeth out of
the mouth of God,

MATT. 4:4

Take time . . .

1. Take time to always be at the crossroads in the lives of your children, whether they be six or sixteen.

2. Take time to be a real friend to your children.

3. Take time to read to your children. . . .

4. Take time to pray with your children.

5. Take time to have a meaningful weekly home evening. Make this one of your great family traditions.

6. Take time to be together at mealtimes as often as possible.

7. Take time daily to read the scriptures together as a family.

8. Take time to do things together as a family.

9. Take time to teach your children.

10. Take the time to truly love your children. A mother's unqualified love approaches Christ-like love.

THOMAS S. MONSON, "MEMORIES OF YESTERDAY, COUNSEL FOR TODAY," Ensign, MAY 1992, 4

Take especial care of your family . . .

D&C 126:3

Maybe it is time for us to think of
turning the hearts of the parents to children
now while living in order that,
after they are gone to the beyond,
there might be that bond
between parents and children
which will last beyond death.

HAROLD B. LEE

God is the designer of the family. He intended that the greatest of happiness, the most satisfying aspects of life, the deepest joys should come in our association together and our concerns one for another as father and mother and child.

GORDON B. HINCKLEY, "WHAT GOD HATH JOINED TOGETHER," *Ensign,* MAY 1991, 74

...he did heal them every one...

3 NE. 17:9

Little children
are precious
to our Father in
Heaven.

HE LOVES THEM AND LOOKS AFTER THEM WITH THE SAME TENDER CARE NO MATTER WHERE THEY LIVE OR HOW THEY DRESS OR LOOK. HE LOVES THE DARK, CURLY-HAIRED FIJIAN, AND THE KIND, GAILY DRESSED CHILDREN IN SAMOA AND TONGA AND TAHITI WHO WEAR LAVALAVAS AND RUN BAREFOOT ON THEIR WARM LAND OF THE SOUTH SEAS. HE LOVES THE LITTLE ENGLISH BOYS AND GIRLS WHO ALL DRESS ALIKE AT SCHOOL IN THEIR SHORT PANTS, SHIRTS, AND TIES, OR SKIRTS AND SWEATERS. HE LOVES THE CHILDREN IN JAPAN, WHO WEAR WESTERNIZED CLOTHES AND ALWAYS REMOVE THEIR SHOES WHEN THEY ENTER THE CHAPEL. HE LOVES THE SUN-TANNED CHILDREN IN SOUTH AMERICA WHO EAT TORTILLAS WITH ALL THEIR MEALS, AND THE LAMANITES WITH THEIR BRIGHTLY COLORED BEADS AND THEIR ANCIENT CEREMONIAL DANCES.

OUR FATHER LOVES HIS CHILDREN EVERYWHERE.

HOWARD W. HUNTER, "FRIEND TO FRIEND," *Friend*, OCT. 1971, 10;
SPENCER W. KIMBALL, "THE GOSPEL OF REPENTANCE," *Ensign*, OCT. 1982, 2

Wherefore, whithersoever they shall send you, go ye, and I will be with you;

and in whatsoever place ye shall proclaim my name

an effectual door shall be opened unto you, that they may receive my word.

D&C 112:19

WHAT DID THE MASTER SPEND HIS LIFE DOING? HE WAS JUST A TEACHER, TEACHING HUMAN SOULS, INSPIRING THEM TO LIVE RIGHTEOUSLY. THERE IS NO HIGHER CALLING THAN THAT. WHETHER IT BE DONE IN THE MISSION FIELD OR HERE AT HOME WITH A GROUP IN A PRIMARY CLASS, THEY ARE ALL ETERNAL SOULS THAT WE WORK WITH.

EZRA TAFT BENSON, *The Teachings of Ezra Taft Benson* (SALT LAKE CITY: BOOKCRAFT, 1988), 306

. . . . be of good cheer;
I have overcome the world.

JOHN 16:33